HOME SELLING
TRUTHS
AND REAL ESTATE
MYTHS

THE ESSENTIAL GUIDE FOR
FIRST-TIME HOME SELLERS

TRACI OLIVER

ARCHWAY
PUBLISHING

Archway Publishing books may be ordered through booksellers or by contacting:

Archway Publishing
1663 Liberty Drive
Bloomington, IN 47403
www.archwaypublishing.com
1 (888) 242-5904

ISBN: 978-1-4808-5944-9 (sc)
ISBN: 978-1-4808-5945-6 (e)

Library of Congress Control Number: 2018903508

Print information available on the last page.

Archway Publishing rev. date: 03/29/2018

Acknowledgement

Real estate is more of a lifestyle than a career for me. It is early phone calls and late night contract discussing. It is urgent situations during the dinner hour or last minute changes to a schedule to accommodate others. Helping my clients navigate the sale or purchase of their largest investment and most personal space is a responsibility I don't take lightly. Every sale is someone's most important transaction.

The agents that work with me on my real estate team have the same work ethic, commitment to excellence and love for real estate. Both Andie Cunningham and Beth Walsh are true professionals and an asset to my real estate business. Thank you both for your additional help with this project. Taking the overwhelmingly detailed process of preparing and selling a home from real life to a condensed format that can be expressed on paper was made possible with your helpful involvement.

My expertise comes from successfully closing hundreds of transactions. Each and every one of those unique transactions has provided the experience and knowledge that is the basis of what I offer my clients today as well as the information in this book. Every family I have helped through the years stands out in my memory and I am forever grateful to each of my past clients for the opportunity to help them with their most important transaction.

Finally, I greatly appreciate the sacrifices my own family has made through the years. Being available to my clients means sometimes being unavailable to my family. Thank you to my husband and daughter for your understanding that I may not work all the time, but I am always working.

Contents

Introduction

For most home sellers, the property they are selling is one of - if not THE - most expensive assets they own. Through the years I have worked with first time sellers at various stages of their lives, yet this is almost always the case.

Despite the magnitude of this transaction and the lack of first-hand experience, many home owners approach selling their home less prepared than they should or could be. Over the course of hundreds of transactions representing sellers at various price-points, I have found that the same questions, concerns and misunderstandings about the process of selling a home frequently arise.

My purpose in writing this book is to offer a comprehensive understanding of the importance of preparation, market analysis, professional marketing, unemotional negotiating, transaction management, unexpected problem-solving and the knowledge that more goes into a successful sale that is visible from the surface.

Every seller wants top dollar. Every buyer want a deal. A good real estate agent can help a seller achieve the former while the buyer believes the latter.

The information in this book is intended for any seller to better understand the process of selling a home. Because every real estate market is different and each home is unique, the information should be considered as broad information that may or may not be useful to your specific situation or typical in your market. I recommend consulting a local real estate professional to discuss your individual needs and to best consult you about your specific real estate market.

Chapter One

Be Ready and Committed to Selling

"When you're interested, you do what is convenient. When you're committed, you do whatever it takes"

- John Assaraf

If you are not committed or motivated to sell your home, don't. That is probably not what you would expect to hear from someone in the business of selling homes or the first statement in a book about the home selling process, but this is probably the single most important advice a potential seller can pick up from this book. Let me break down the four simple reasons:

1. The actions you will need to undertake to get your home truly market-ready for a successful sale will be a tremendous amount of work and possibly cost.

2. Once your home is on the market, you will be opening your most private space - your home - to total strangers and usually at their convenience.
3. The entire process will be highly stressful and extremely disruptive to you and your family's daily routine, including a lack of control over the entire timeline.
4. Your home's value is determined by neighborhood sales. If you are not truly ready to sell and stagnate on the market, you will actually aid in the lowering of the overall value of your home by unnecessarily altering supply and demand of homes in your neighborhood or price range.

The goal with the above statement is not to paint a negative picture of the home selling process or to scare you from wanting to ever move from your current home. It is important to understand that this is a mighty big undertaking. The point of this chapter is to understand the importance of being ready and committed to selling before you even start.

While that seems like a pretty obvious first step, surprisingly a lot of sellers think that you can "test" the market or be loosely committed to maybe selling their home if they get the right price or under the perfect scenario. "I'm not in a hurry" or "I don't need to move" or countless other non-committal utterings have been heard before. These statements are detrimental to the selling process and signify that the seller if not ready to sell.

Here is the bottom line: If you are not fully committed to selling your home and seeing it through to the end, then don't start the undertaking for your own sanity. Of course, things come up sometimes that changes the course of a sellers actions, but for the point of this conversation let's stick to the need to be "all in" from the beginning. If you are not willing to see the sale to the finish line and do what it takes, then simply don't start.

I will get into great detail as to what it takes and why you need to prepare your home for a successful sale. At this juncture understand that before your home goes on the market, there will be out of pocket costs and certainly time commitments to prepare or repair your home for market. An initial step is to know roughly what those costs will be and what your availability to focus on the endeavor is before you jump in. I've included a generalized worksheet in Appendix II of this book, but a real estate professional will be your best resource in determining these estimated costs, as we will discuss shortly

If work or other life circumstances will not allow you to be all in, then perhaps now is not the right time to sell your home. Often, the stressful act of selling a house seems to dovetail with other major life events like getting married, having children, changing jobs or life events such as divorce or death. The already stressful environment created from these other life happenings can certainly magnify the overwhelming aspects of selling your home for some. Other people find that if life is already chaotic, what does one more thing added to the fire really do? Understanding your own propensity to handle stressful, life changing events will be key to knowing what you can handle personally.

An experienced real estate agent with the knowledge of how to guide you from the beginning is going to be your best ally. Your real estate agent should be able to help you with the necessary resources, creating a time-table and prioritizing what investments you need to make to your home to get it market-ready. At this juncture, you'll also need to have a general idea of your home's market value, as well as the estimated costs of selling such as fees, taxes and other expenses typical in your specific market. While I will discuss the role a good real estate agent should play throughout the book and in detail later, it is important to form a relationship early so you can stay on task and have a professional guide you through this crucial initial phase of determining what your costs of selling vs potential net profit look like in addition to guiding you on the right way to prepare your home for market.

Where Will I Go Next?

An early decision and important component of the home selling process is to ask yourself "where will you live once your home sells?" Obviously, if you know you are buying a new home, relocating for your job, or getting married and moving in with your future spouse then you've got this part of the equation down. If you haven't given that next step thought yet, this is key information to have figured out well before you make the commitment to sell your current home.

Jumping ahead in the timeline to once your home is under contract with the new buyer, you will have a limited time frame for you and all of your belongings to be completely out of your home. It is important to note that the actual amount of time from contract to transfer of ownership to new buyer varies from one real estate market to the next and is typically something you can negotiate to some extent.

Selling your current home and buying a new home is a bit of a "chicken or the egg scenario" for many sellers as it is hard to figure out on your own which to do first. Most sellers would like to have the flexibility to find their new home without being worried about selling their existing home. At the same time, if selling their current home is required to buy their new home, it is reasonable to be worried about finding a home within a short timeframe or having to move twice.

There is not an easy answer to this puzzle. Each seller's situation is different and many factors – the present real estate market, type of home they are buying, flexibility of the other seller, marketability of their existing home – go into influencing what sequence of events would work best for a seller. An experienced real estate agent along with a good lender will be able to help you determine the best timeline based on your particular needs and provide options that may work best for you. All the reason to form the valuable relationships early in the process to know all of your options and to have a plan

Some options that may be available in your market include:

- Renting-back (commonly called a "Post-Settlement Occupancy")
  Here the seller stays in the home after the exchange of ownership and essentially "rents" their own home back from the purchasers after closing for a brief period of time (usually limited by purchaser's lender to 90 days or less) and pays the purchaser's actual per diem carrying costs as a credit back to the purchaser.

- Seller "Home of Choice" Contingency
  This is a contingency that the seller controls, allowing the contract to be subject to the seller finding their "home of choice". This allows the seller to void the

contract within a set period of time should they not be able to find a suitable home.

Both of these scenarios, if options in your specific markets, require a very flexible buyer and possibly limits your home as an option for many other buyers. While strategies like these give the seller more control over their timeline, these are buyer obstacles and further reduces the marketability of your home and likely your ability to negotiate on more important factors such as price.

If you are purchasing another home in conjunction with selling your current home (commonly referred to as buying and selling simultaneously), the biggest question to ask is whether or not you can afford to buy your next home before you sell your current home. This question is best answered by a qualified lender that has reviewed your creditworthiness and has looked at your specific situation – not an online mortgage calculator – but working with a lender to review your entire financial picture in light of current lending requirements. Knowing approximately what your home can possibly sell for and your estimated net proceeds will be information your real estate agent can provide. All of this information should be reviewed as part of your overall selling and buying plan. Only then can you work with your real estate agent to determine your best strategy and timeline.

A few options that some sellers consider when selling and buying simultaneously include:

- Buying Contingent on Selling
  This is when you make your home purchase subject to you being able to sell your current home. This requires the seller to agree to the possibility that

you may not be able to sell your home and risks the buyer not being able to sell and thus not being able to move forward with new home. In a seller's market or if the seller's timeline does not allow, this option is not usually available.

- Sell Then Buy – The Interim Move
Some sellers prefer to sell first, have the money in the bank and then start the hunt for a new home. This involves moving twice and finding a short-term housing option, but allows a seller to move at a more controlled pace, know exactly how much they will net from their home sale and separates the process into two manageable transactions.

- Buy Then Sell – The Risk Taker
For the very well qualified buyer with lender approvals and an understanding and budget to carry two mortgages for an indefinite time – this option allows a buyer to get into their home of choice and then be able to sell their home without the inconvenience of living in it at the time. This of course comes with a higher financial risk as market conditions can rapidly change.

Because every seller's situation is unique, it is best for you and your real estate agent to work as a team to determine the best option for you. Mapping out a plan and having a back-up plan is crucial in determining the timeline of your current home's sale. Your real estate agent will let you know what is typical in your current market and how these choices may impact your ability to sell.

Buying and selling at the same time is a complicated series of steps. If you were to step back and actually look at all that needs to happen simultaneously, you'd wonder how anyone ever buys and sells their homes. The potential for transactions to fall like dominoes is avoidable with careful planning and knowing what your options are before you get started.

Being prepared for anything you do in life will net the best results. A real estate transaction involves many moving parts, multiple outside influences, a tremendous amount of money and legal ramifications. It is crucial you align yourself with professionals that are licensed and do this for a living as well as be realistic in your expectations.

Chapter Two

Yes, You Really Do Need to Hire a Real Estate Professional

"If you think it's expensive to hire a professional to do the job, wait until you hire an amateur."

- Red Adair

Selecting an agent and agent roles

A good agent is a marketing pro, a fierce negotiator, a communication hub, an organized manager, a timeline coordinator and able to stay ahead of every step along the way to be advanced lookout for potential icebergs and offer proactive solutions to stop a sinking sale.

Real estate agents are required to be licensed and are governed by local and state boards. Every state has very specific agency laws - restrictions and requirements pertaining to how a real estate agent represents sellers as well as buyers for that matter. I won't get into the specifics here since this important information varies from state to state. The real estate professional you choose to work with will carefully explain how your state classifies agency roles.

What this chapter will highlight is the importance of selecting a listing agent that will represent you – the seller – throughout your most important transaction. In the previous chapter we covered the significance of involving a real estate agent early on in the process for initial guidance and planning. Selecting a real estate agent early on will aide in creating a comprehensive plan, have expert advice to make key decisions that may otherwise cause problems later and to get the most bang for your buck!

The planning, marketing and selling of what may very well be your largest asset requires a skill set honed from years of experience across a multitude of market situations. Many components of a home sale are beyond a seller's control, while others require decisions that not only could affect the amount a home sells for, but whether the home sells at all in some cases. A capable real estate agent will be able to properly guide the seller and manage all aspects of the process from the planning and pre-market stage up to the completion of the sale.

It is probably helpful to understand what a real estate agent actually does. Like any other service business, you will find that different agents offer varying levels of service and a variety of different approaches to how they will market your home.

At bare minimum, there are three primary services most, if not all, real estate agents provide:

- Exposure in your area's Multiple Listing Service (or MLS as it is commonly referred to)
- Real Estate Lockbox Access
- Signage

The Multiple Listing Service (MLS) is your local Real Estate Board's database of available properties. While this is only accessed by licensed real estate agents, the MLS acts as the hub from which most online sources and real estate websites obtain the information about your property. It is commonly understood that your real estate agent will enter your home into the MLS, thus sending the information out to numerous mediums to reach all of the potential buyers.

Access – or the ability for your home to be shown to potential buyers is (pardon the pun) key to your ultimate success. Your real estate agent will likely provide access through a lockbox used only by licensed professionals in your local MLS area. This system both controls and simplifies access to your home.

The classic "for sale" sign is also a standard-issue offering that allows the world - or at least those venturing past your home - to know you are on the market.

The breadth of services offered will vary enormously from agent to agent – and these nuances will likely result in the reason why you select one agent over another to represent you. Below is a very generalized list of some of the additional services a seller should expect from their real estate agent:

- Premarketing preparation advice and staging
- Market condition comprehension and comparable sale information
- Pricing recommendations

- Marketing Plan, Photography and Marketing Materials
- Management of showings and feedback
- Negotiation of offers
- Facilitation of appropriate and required paperwork and documentation
- Management of transaction and interface with lenders, inspectors, title agents, etc.
- Trouble shooting possible issues to get the transaction to the closing table

How to find your best agent

Just as you would seek the best surgeon or car mechanic, researching the perfect real estate agent for your most valuable asset should be a careful vetting process. Most real estate agents are independent contractors or self-employed. As sales professionals, you will discover that as a group real estate agents are excellent marketers of themselves. While someone who markets themselves well will likely also market your property well, be sure to verify experience and credentials.

Recommendations from friends or co-workers is always a good place to start. Another unique opportunity is to visit open houses and meet prospective agents "on-the-job" so to speak or to call listing agents from their signs pretending to be a prospective buyer to get a feel for how they would represent your home to a buyer. Most of the major online real estate sites have reviews posted by previous sellers and link to actual recent transactions so you can see how many homes each agent has listed and sold in your area.

Because of the size of your transaction, I recommend interviewing more than one real estate agent. You will find that there are a variety of different business models, as well as different approaches to marketing and selling your home. Once you have found one or more agents to consider, here are some suggested questions to ask during the interview process:

- Are you a full time agent?
- How long have you been selling real estate full time?
- How many transactions do you complete per year?
- What percentage of your transactions are listings vs buyer-side sales?
- Have you sold in this price range, location, and neighborhood?
- How will you market my home differently?
- What makes you a good negotiator?
- Will you help stage or provide a stager?
- What do your marketing materials/photography look like?
- What is your list price to sold price average?
- What is your "days on market" average?
- What is the communication plan and frequency throughout transaction?
- How do you support the transaction after an offer is accepted?
- Do you have online reviews and can you provide recent seller references?

It is important that you feel comfortable in communicating with your real estate agent throughout the transaction. You will have many questions during the various stages of the selling process and you should be able to comfortably ask without feeling like a bother. There is a lot more that goes into selling a home than most first-time sellers realize and will often need to clarify the same information more than once. Your agent should know the answers to your basic questions and be able to explain what to expect while your home is on the market and then be able to guide you through each step along the way up to settlement or closing.

You are hiring an expert to oversee the selling of your largest investment, so you should have confidence in their ability and experience first and foremost. In addition, you will be spending a great deal of time with your agent over the course of your transaction, so compatibility will be key to developing a professional relationship.

Chapter Three

Wait, I Think I Can
Sell this Myself

"Price is what you pay. Value is what you get."

- Warren Buffet

While everyone wants to save money, first time sellers especially should take a step back to fully understand what they are trading in exchange for the assumed savings and the risks of going it alone.

Of course, selling your home without a real estate agent is a possible option for some sellers. In fact, choosing to take the "For Sale By Owner" (or FSBO as they are commonly called in the industry) is possibly why many of you are reading this book.

While considering this path, there are two important facts you need to consider:

FACT #1: An incredibly small percentage of homes sell without the use of a listing agent

FSBOs accounted for only 8% of home sales in 2015 ~ *Source:* 2016 National Association of REALTORS® Profile of Home Buyers and Sellers

FACT #2: FSBOs sell their homes for less money than Real Estate Agent sold homes

FSBO home sold for an average of 23% less than agent-assisted home sales. The average price of a FSBO was $185,000 to the agent-assisted $240,000 sales price ... that is a $60,000 difference. ~ *Source:* 2016 National Association of REALTORS® Profile of Home Buyers and Sellers

2015 Home Sale Prices

Agent Assisted Home Sale Price

FSBO Home Sale Price

23% Less

Let that marinate for a moment: of the millions of real estate transactions sold annually, only a small percent take on this enormous task without the services of licensed professional AND in turn those sellers on average make less money in selling their homes than their counterparts who hired a professional to represent them.

Falling on Your Own Sword

Most seasoned sellers that have sold a home previously understand the enormous time commitment involved in the selling process. Then there is the incredible difficulty in separating the intimacy of this sale not only being their personal home, but also their largest financial investment. Very few people can detach themselves from the emotional component of selling their own personal possession. You do have to have a thick skin to sell your home. A real estate agent acts as a buffer, protecting the seller from feedback and uncomfortable conversations. Most sellers are not equipped or experienced to negotiate on their own behalf. They are simply too close to the transaction making it difficult to not let emotions factor into their decisions.

Real estate transactions are stressful in nature and involve larger amounts of money than most people deal with on a regular basis. You are working with people on both sides of the transaction who are typically close to their breaking point in terms of stress. Experienced sellers have learned that there is always the potential for the unknown and the unexpected. Most real estate agents can recount countless stories of how they resolved situations in every transaction that a seller would have never been aware of and/or able to deal with on their own.

As a first time seller you simply don't know what you don't know! A professional real estate agent, however, deals with the processes, issues and demands of selling a home every single day.

A true professional makes it look easy - that is why they are successful. Whether a pastry chef, a figure skater, a guitar virtuoso, professional athlete or master carpenter - these professionals make an otherwise difficult and challenging skill look so easy that anyone can do it. The internet is full of DIY and Pinterest "fails" to prove otherwise.

Spend Money to Make Money?

For the FSBO seller, it is all about the money. There is simply no other reason to go this alone other than the hopes of saving a few dollars. As mentioned in the first chapter, there are actual costs to selling a home. Many of these costs are inescapable such as paying off mortgage liens, taxes and recording or title search fees. These are the costs of doing business and important to understand as you calculate your total selling costs.

The expense of hiring a real estate agent, however, is a cost that FSBO sellers *believe* to be nonessential. THIS is the driving force for most FSBOs as they seek to pocket this great savings by going it alone. And on paper this seems like a brilliant idea.

The truth is that while focusing on **COST**, the FSBO seller is overlooking the importance of the **VALUE** that will have more impact on their final **NET**. The final net proceeds to the seller should be the most important number.

Since the above referenced research study data shows that transactions sold by a real estate agent typically sell at a higher price, the FSBO seller would be better to increase their "costs" by a small percentage to "net" a higher final sales price which would then absorb the additional nominal "cost". By looking only at the cost savings, the typical FSBO seller is often being short-sighted.

So why does the research show FSBOs sell for less than homes listed by a professional or even not sell at all? These factors are what historically doom the FSBO seller:

- The FSBO will historically overprice their homes
- They have a more limited exposure to willing and able buyers
- Poor property condition and/or ability to access home for showing factors
- Lack of the professional resources at every stage of the process
- Transactions that fall apart due to inexperience and never make it to the closing table

Who Really Owns The Savings?

The biggest factor to the lower FSBO sales prices is the hijacking of the seller's anticipated savings. The FSBO seller sets out with the intention of saving the cost of hiring a professional. The savvy buyer, however, will end up "owning" the very cost savings the FSBO seller traveled this path in hopes of pocketing. In fact, most FSBO sellers don't even realize they are giving up their equity in the transaction.

Let me explain:

The seller markets their home as an FSBO. The interested buyer will almost always without fail deduct the buyer's estimate of the FSBO seller "saved" overhead from their offer. What was supposed to be the seller's windfall, becomes the benefit to the buyer. The seller in turn "nets" nearly the same by selling his home lower with the estimated fees adjusted from the sales price as he would selling at market value or higher with a professional. The seller is walking away with the same net proceeds – or less as indicated in the study – only without the many benefits of representation and professional guidance that often proves to be priceless in many transactions.

An experienced professional will better prepare and price your property, create more demand, be in a better position to negotiate on your behalf and manage your transaction to avoid the proverbial camel back-breaking straw that you never saw coming. All of this is priceless when it statistically nets you a higher price for your home than you could get on your own.

Chapter Four

Preparation, Decluttering and Staging

"Before anything else, preparation is the key to success"

\- Alexander Graham Bell

I often say if I can get in front of a seller 1-2 years before they are ready to sell, the home will be truly ready for market and we can expect a highly successful sale. That amount of advanced planning and preparation is not always possible and the timeline is typically shorter, but know that it is never too early to start preparing your home.

There are three P's to a successful home sale:

1. Preparation
2. Promotion
3. Price

Preparation is a Priority

Your home will be the new buyer's most important purchase and to them it is also likely a sizeable investment. Before a buyer even walks into your home, they have typically set the bar fairly high for themselves. They have made a list of what they want in their next home and what they are willing to pay to get that. Their expectations are that the home they decide to buy will be upgraded to market conditions, squeaky clean, in good repair and move-in condition.

Most buyers are not willing to make financial sacrifices to make the condition of your home work for them. In fact, the typical buyer cannot see past clutter or disrepair, and typically are not looking to do the hard work to get your home up to their standards. This is especially true for the buyer willing to pay top price or even market value.

Unless you are selling your home as a below market-value distress sale or as a "fixer-upper" (which is an entirely different conversation) then the answer to the question you are about to ask is: YES, you have to invest time, sweat equity and possibly money to properly prepare your home for sale.

I like to enlist the analogy that buying a home is a little like dating or going on a job interview. When a buyer first visits your home, this is your one and only first impression opportunity. You certainly want that buyer to like you and, even better, to have some interest in you. You wouldn't show up to a first date or a job interview in dirty sweat pants and unbathed any more than you should allow potential buyers to see a messy or overly personalized home. You only get one first impression with potential buyers. Properly preparing your home before you go on the market and maintaining your home to always look its best for each showing is an absolute must for success when selling.

Preparation, decluttering and staging are three key steps in getting your home on the market. These are time consuming tasks for a seller, but know that the effort made here will directly affect your ability to sell your home on average faster and for more money.

According to the National Association of Realtors 2017 Profile of Home Staging Report:

- 77% of buyers' agents say that staging makes it easier for buyers to visualize the property as their future home
- 49% of buyers' agents say that staging a home increases the dollar value offered
- 62% of sellers' agents say that staging a home decreases the amount of time a home spends on the market

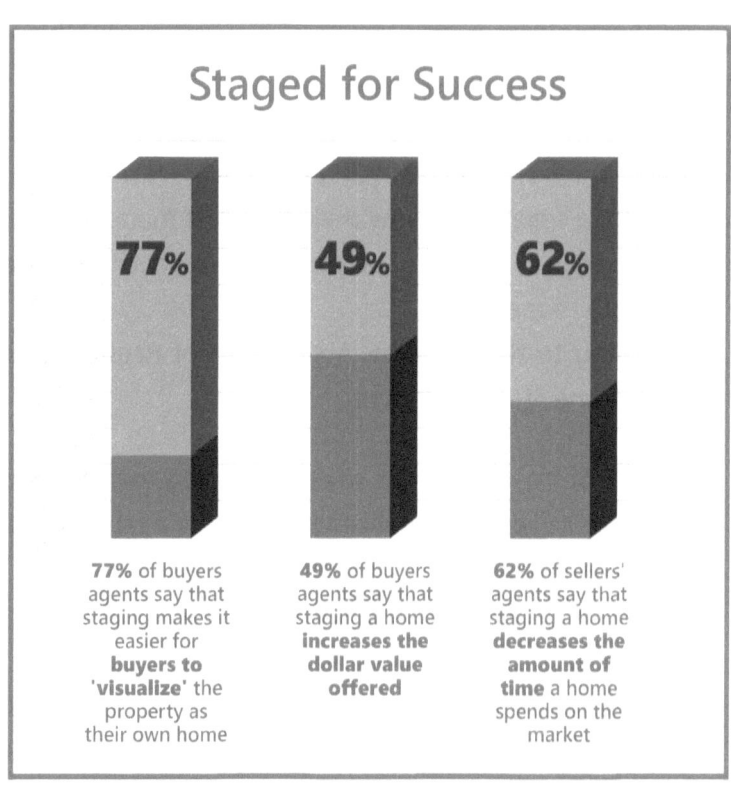

Staged for Success

77% of buyers agents say that staging makes it easier for **buyers to 'visualize'** the property as their own home

49% of buyers agents say that staging a home **increases the dollar value offered**

62% of sellers' agents say that staging a home **decreases the amount of time** a home spends on the market

Good Repair Shows You Care

It is clearly understood that no seller wants to put excessive time and money into a home they are selling, but for your home to be a contender you are going to have to bring it up to playing level if needed. First rule of home preparation is that the home needs to be in overall good repair. That means anything not working needs to work, anything broken needs to be repaired, anything missing needs to be replaced, and so on. When it comes to upgrading a kitchen or bath, replacing carpet or major systems - those are case by case scenarios that need to factor in the market, the type of home and the price range – you should consult with your real estate professional who best knows your market. Good working order and clean will always trump upgraded, but keep in mind that careful attention to pricing will come into play if your home does not have the upgraded features or newer components that similar homes have. As every real estate market is different and in some states sellers are required to disclose know defects, previous defects and a history of repairs - please consult your real estate professional on the proper course of action when making repairs and consider the information here as general advice only.

One of my favorite examples of pre-market seller correction is when there is a case of "Color Shock Block". This is when an otherwise neutral room with an unusual, dated or highly personalized carpet color, wall color or even cabinet or appliance color will stop buyers from looking further. That one feature becomes a negativity that overshadows all of the good things your home has to offer. In fact, those redeeming qualities are often never noticed as buyers cannot get past the distracting eye sore. Online, your home becomes the "orange house" or the "wallpaper ceiling house" and if you are lucky enough to get buyers to walk through your home, all they remember is that one thing that could have been easily corrected BEFORE you went on the market. A small cost upfront is an investment in the sale-ability of your home. In the rare case that a buyer can look past a negative feature, their cost estimate to fix is usually higher than what you could have done it for. The buyer will lower the value of the home AND factor in the cost of the paint or carpet.

Maximize When You Neutralize

The magic word in home preparation is neutral! A clean palate that blends effortlessly and doesn't shock, contrast, clash or offend will appeal to far more buyers. A neutral home allows the features, square footage and potential of a home to standout. A good analogy is if you were to serve ice cream to a fairly large group, odds are vanilla would be a flavor most guests would enjoy. Something along the lines of Pistachio may appeal to a small handful of guests, but the majority of folks would likely pass and choose to not have any ice cream at all. Your neutral décor is the Vanilla ice cream of real estate home preparations. Pistachio is that crazy green carpet in the family room that will likely not appeal to many buyers and they will move along to their next choice.

When I consult with my sellers on our pre-market preparation plan, we walk room-by-room with a yellow pad and pen in hand. I am looking for what needs to be repaired or replaced first (preparation), then we break down what needs to be removed (decluttered) and then how the room's features will be best be shown and the negatives downplayed (staging). The reality is that "stuff" comes into our homes but never leaves on its own. Only when a seller is faced with moving does decluttering go from something you should do to something you now have to do. Every seller dreads this part, but back to the commitment to the selling process we discussed earlier - if you are moving then all of your stuff needs to move too! Do it on the front end when it will benefit you the most.

I know there are skeptics out there - I run into them all the time. As we discussed in Chapter 1, you need to be committed to selling your home before entering the process. Prepping and staging your home to show its best is one of the seller's biggest and most important initiatives to have the results desired. Truth of the matter, this typically is not costly in dollars, but in the time to do this the right way. In the end this is an important investment in your home that will reward you with a strong sale. The end game is you are selling square footage. The less stuff crammed in every nook and cranny you have in your home, the more home a potential buyer can see. In turn, the home is less about you and your stuff and the future owner can see not only the features of the home, but can visualize their belongings and themselves in the space.

Any experienced real estate agent can recount buyer after buyer rejecting an otherwise perfect match of home simply because of how it showed. Emotions factor into every buyer's decision - this will be their home after all. Very few buyers can see the "potential" in a home that does not show well or is in need of repairs. Those rare buyers that are willing to look past a less prepared home are also savvy enough to know that the price should match the condition. If the buyer is going to do the heavy lifting to fix up your home, they will likely not being paying you for the privilege. Successful sellers need to invest time, money or both into the product they are selling.

Good Bye Clutter. Hello Square Footage

Decluttering and staging go hand-in-hand to create an emotional response while at the same time highlighting the selling features of your home and downplaying the less desirable attributes. Not in an attempt to be deceptive, but to shine a light on features buyers love such as removing area rugs to show hardwood floors or opening blinds to highlight sunny breakfast areas. Staging can make the negative features less prominent such as clearing out extra coats when there is limited closet space or remove larger furniture when a particular room is smaller. The goal is to showcase the positive attributes of the home.

How you live in a home is quite different than how you need to show the features of the home. For example, I imagine your family room is beautifully decorated with overstuffed furniture that not only makes the room cozy, but also allows the maximum number of people to gather around the huge jumbo Tron of a television you have mounted on the wall conveniently positioned next to all of your audio visual and gaming components. As the perfect host, you have an enormous coffee table so that your halftime spread can be enjoyed in all its glory and everyone has a place to put their drink (on a coaster of course!). Further the wall of spectacular windows has been attractively covered with wood blinds that are closed to avoid the glare on aforementioned television and the floating shelves so carefully mounted above the sofa feature matching framed photos of all the important people and events you hold dear.

To properly show the selling features of your home to a potential buyer, this room would need to have the blinds open, photos and likely shelves removed with the corresponding holes filled, the furniture reduced down to a couple pieces arranged so the room can be accessed and seen and the center of the room being the fireplace or windows, not the TV. This "redo" is not how any of us (including the future buyer) will live in the room, but exactly how the room needs to be showcased to highlight the features.

A good realtor can guide you as to what needs to stay or go in your own home and whether or not staging with rented furniture is needed. I often suggest renting a storage unit or using a portable storage solution to move out non-essential items while on the market. The silver lining is that once your home sells, you will need to pack everything at that time. The preparation, decluttering and staging process allows you to "pre pack" getting you ahead of a pretty big task that lies ahead in the selling and moving process.

Chapter Five

Price it Wrong, it Stays on Too Long!

"Nowadays people know the price of everything and the value of nothing."

- Oscar Wilde

What is it worth to a buyer?

Of the quotes throughout this book, this one above is most interesting as Oscar Wilde died in 1900 - long before the internet and the endless flow of information became available to today's consumers. While Mr. Wilde was not speaking of modern life, he sums up perfectly what every seller will face in today's real estate environment: consumers will already know what your home is worth to them BEFORE they ever step foot inside.

The pricing component of selling a home is overwhelming to most sellers. Further complicating matters is that many are confused by the different forms of value for the same home.

- Listing Price
  the amount a seller determines their home is worth based on market conditions and is the price at which their home is listed for sale.

- Market Value
  essentially what your home is worth to a buyer at a given time, typically based on the value of other similar homes they are comparing your home to and supply vs demand.

- Appraised Value
  an opinion of value given to your home from an independent appraiser based on market conditions and features of your home in comparison to other similar sold properties.

- Assessed Value
  the amount the government taxing authority uses to determine the amount of your real estate property tax assessment.

Determining the listing price of your home is of critical importance to a successful sale, yet is probably the most difficult step along the journey of selling your home. The successful seller will look to find a listing price that can be supported by market value and easily confirmed by appraised value.

Let's start by understanding who "owns" the decision of what your home is worth. Listing agents and sellers may be in the position of setting the listing or sales price, but buyers ultimately determine market value or what they are willing to pay for what is essentially a commodity.

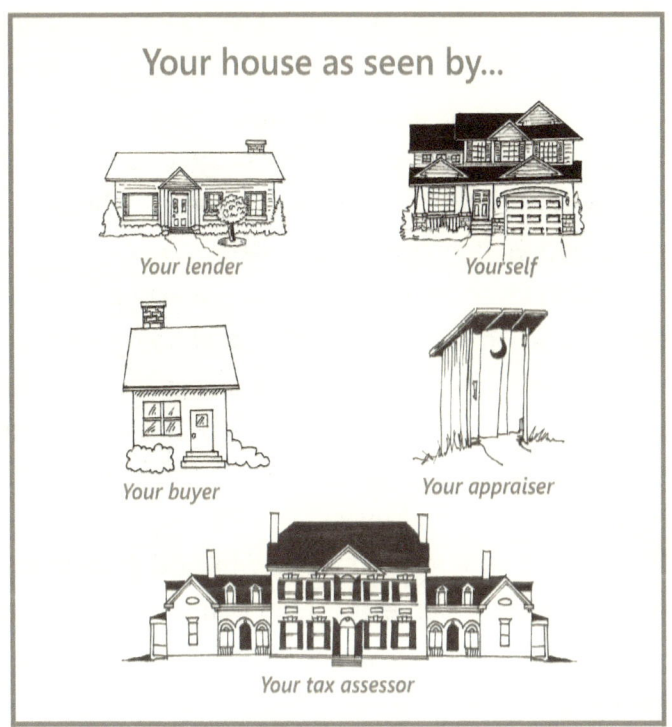

Your house as seen by...

Your lender

Yourself

Your buyer

Your appraiser

Your tax assessor

You see, your home is not the only home on the market at any given time. What's more, buyers have likely seen other homes over the course of their home search that they will use as their basis for determining your home's value from their perspective. It is often said the beauty is in the eye of the beholder. When it comes to determining the value of a home, the ultimate test is to ask "what is this home worth to a buyer?"

The difficulty in pricing is that no two homes are ever exactly alike. Whereas an article of clothing, the latest electronic gadget or a share of stock can all compare their value based on what the "going rate" is at that particular moment in time, your home has other factors to consider.

What is important to understand, and one of the hardest for most sellers to process, is that not every improvement, upgrade or advantage your home has over the competition will actually add value to your home. Upgraded kitchens and baths, new hardwood flooring, new windows or heating systems, finished vs unfinished basements, garages vs no garages, backing to woods vs backing to highway, deck or patio vs neither, larger square footage vs smaller home are some of the examples of the type of improvements or advantages that do factor into real value. Decorative, personalized, custom or specific improvements may have cost a bundle to a seller, but may not be of value to a buyer.

Some improvements add value, while others add to the overall value of your home, meaning that for example painting your entire home that was in need of painting may not recoup dollar for dollar of your investment in a higher sales price, but does make the home appealing to more buyers and therefore aids in the home selling at the best possible price.

It should also be noted that there are many outside factors that impact the price such as inventory or how many other homes are on the market at the same time, interest rates and market favorability. This is why your home may not be able to sell for the same price your neighbor sold if they sold in a previous year, for example.

Why is Price Such A Big Deal?

Of everything that goes into selling your home, properly pricing it from the start is without a doubt, the top factor in determining the best possible outcome for a seller – which is

---

typically selling for the highest possible price in a reasonable timeframe.

Let's face it, most sellers want top dollar for their home. Conventional thinking would be to then price it high to achieve that goal. On the surface that seems logical, however that is not how the real estate market typically works. In fact, that approach is contraindicative as overpriced homes are difficult to sell.

To understand why a strategy of pricing your home higher than market value may backfire, let's look at a few facts about selling real estate:

1. Buyers shopping in the price range your home is worth, will not see your home and will buy other homes.
2. A higher priced home will be compared to correctly homes in same price range, which will likely offer more value.
3. An overpriced home sends a message that the seller is not serious about selling, therefore buyers skip seeing it not wanting to waste their time and risk missing out on more viable homes.
4. By the time you lower price to be realistic, you've missed willing and able buyers and now have to wait for new buyers to come on the market.
5. The longer a home sits on the market, the less it will sell for as it becomes a "stale" listing and is passed up for newer, well priced homes.

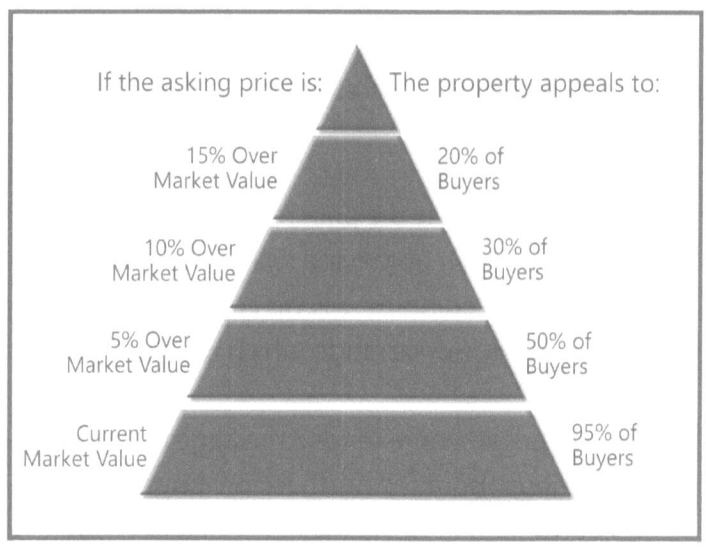

If the asking price is:

15% Over Market Value — 20% of Buyers

10% Over Market Value — 30% of Buyers

5% Over Market Value — 50% of Buyers

Current Market Value — 95% of Buyers

The property appeals to:

Pricing your home higher than market value will dramatically decrease the amount of buyer traffic and interest, whereas pricing closer to or at market value will generate the highest amount of traffic and interest

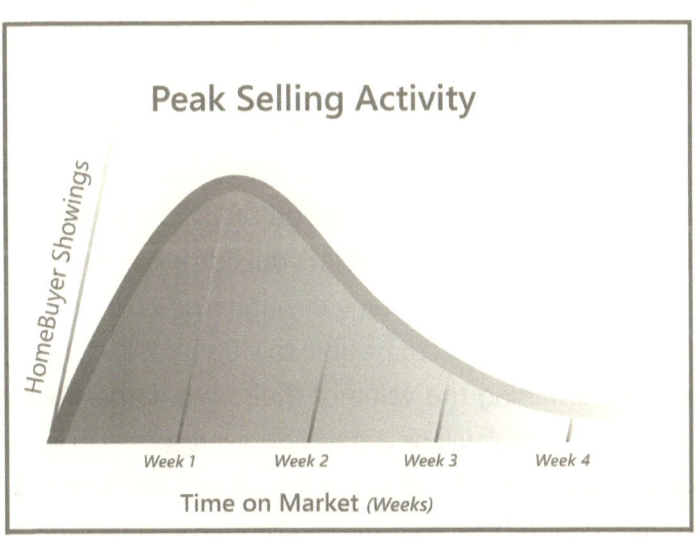

Peak Selling Activity

HomeBuyer Showings

Week 1   Week 2   Week 3   Week 4

Time on Market *(Weeks)*

You will receive the most traffic and interest to your home when you first go on the market. As buyers pass you by, you are then in a position of waiting for new buyers to enter the marketplace.

So how do I come up with the right price?

Properly pricing a home is a honed skill that requires an understanding of the current market and how that home fits into that market from a buyer's perspective. This is important to emphasize because what a seller would like or needs to net from the sale of their home is not relevant to the actual value of that home to a buyer. So many times I have encountered a seller with a number in mind – typically based on what they would like to make from the sale, what they need for the down payment on their next home or based on what they paid for their home. I would encourage you to re-read chapter one if you think you are this seller, otherwise, understand that a home's value is based on factors outside a seller's needs.

Sellers often see their home through rose-colored glasses. They are too "invested" to be able to step back and be objective in determining the value of their own home. Your real estate professional will be a tremendous resource in guiding your through the pricing process and will be able to help you understand how your home compares to recently sold properties. Typically "current" market data consists of homes like yours that have sold within the past 3-6 months or other variables that make-up your local market environment.

Your real estate agent should be able to prepare a market analysis from MLS data and tax records showing comparable sales information to paint an accurate picture of how your home stacks up against the competition. In rare cases - particularly with very unique properties – it is wise to hire an appraiser to provide a formal appraisal of your home to assist in determining the estimate market value prior to listing your home for sale.

Using this data, you and your real estate agent should determine a listing price as close to market value to maximize traffic and interest in your home. As you go on the market, watching market conditions, listening to feedback and staying tuned in to how your sale is going will allow you and your real estate agent to be proactive. Real estate market conditions can change quickly so having a strategy to stay ahead of the market is key should that happen while you are on the market.

And Then There is an Appraisal

One more consideration in pricing is that once you are under contract down the road, your home will need to appraise for the agreed upon sales price as a condition of the buyer's loan. Appraisers will use this same information that you and your real estate agent derived in determining your listing price.

In short, the market data available when you list your home is typically what the appraiser uses in coming up with their appraised value of your home. This is important to keep in mind to avoid pitfalls later in the game. Your home will ultimately be held to the current market value by an appraiser as a final check and balance on pricing. Price it right from the start and you'll have success and avoid issues later.

Chapter Six

Being on the Market

*"It's like driving a car at night: you never see fur-
ther than your headlights, but you can make the
whole trip that way."*

- E. L. Doctorow

When your home is finally ready to go live and be on the market for all the world to see, most sellers are both relieved and
somewhat excited. The good news is that for the most part,
the more arduous and time consuming stage of the process
for the seller is over and your home is now as marketable as
possible. It is at this point after the prepping and staging are
complete that many weary and sleep-deprived sellers fall in
love again with their current home and think for a moment
about not selling. This is when we know the home is ready
for buyers to see it!

Once a home is on the market, most sellers experience an
immediate power shift. The control of the home selling process moves from the seller's column to the potential buyer's

side. Factors such as market conditions, interest rates, weather, your neighbor deciding to put their home on the market and just about everything and anything that can impact your sale. This is certainly the tip of the stress iceberg that most sellers experience in an already draining process.

The good news is that if you have followed the advice provided in previous chapters and have hired a knowledgeable agent to represent and guide you through the home selling process, properly prepared your home and have worked with your agent to price your home correctly in light of current market conditions, you should be on the right path. At this juncture my best advice is: TRUST THE PROCESS!

Your agent likely outlined his or her specific marketing plan to you based on your local real estate market conditions and provided you with the data regarding supply and demand so you know whether you are in a buyer's market, a seller's market or something in between. Keep in mind that real estate markets are fluid and ever changing with many factors contributing to the ebb and flow. Your agent has been key in guiding you up to this point and will be the best resource to get you to the finish line.

Trust the Process!

Buyers ... Beware!

Your home needs exposure to sell. Online and in person. The more potential buyers that see your home, the more success you will have. It truly is a numbers game.

Once your real estate agent enters your property into the Multiple Listing Service or MLS - your local real estate board's database that is the foundation of the property information food chain - your property is most likely fed to numerous on-line portals and will show up in search results, in-boxes, drips, text alerts, posts of potential buyers whose criteria matches that of your home. Friendly reminder: THIS is why it is imperative that your home is priced correctly right out of the gate so you reach the potential buyers for your home as you will want to show up in the cross hairs of the buyers looking for your home.

Depending on where a buyer is in the process is how your freshly listed home will be received in the marketplace:

- "New to the Market Buyers" want to see anything and everything as they are still doing their own market research, figuring out what they can get for their money and possibly even where and what they want to buy.
- "Further Along Buyers" have seen everything out there and are more fine-tuned in what they want, what they don't want and are typically ready to see new potential listings as they come on the market.
- "Specific Needs Buyers" will scrub each new listing and see only those with strong potential in meeting their unique needle-in-a-haystack needs.

In general, buyers will take all of the available homes matching their overall criteria and then make an arbitrary cut to a reasonable amount of homes to actually visit and see in person. Reasons for not making the cut could be outside of seller's control such as missing features or wrong school district, but many times it is an issue of how the home is presented, how it appears or price.

With the goal of getting as much traffic into your home as possible, at this point it should be crystal clear how important the three P's – preparation, promotion and pricing – are in achieving a successful sale.

For the love of Real Estate, let them see your home!

You can only sell your home to one buyer. Just one is all you need. The challenge is knowing which buyer will be "it", so you will want to have as many buyers as possible to see your home so you can make a match.

Any seasoned seller will tell you having your home on the market is tumultuous. You have to keep it "show ready" all of the time because you never know when the right buyer will want to see it. You will also need to leave at inconvenient times because buyers usually want to see your home after work, in the evening at dinner time and on weekends – the time you are usually home. Your daily routine will be disruptive because the smell of cooking or piles of laundry or your pet's presence may turn potential buyers away.

While there are boundaries and processes to control access to your home – all of which your real estate agent will work with you to manage – to maximize your exposure and get your home sold you do have to make your home available to be seen by buyers … lots of buyers.

Getting a buyer to visit and tour your home is not as simple as plunking a sign in your yard. As noted previously, buyers have done their homework and are increasingly particular in what they want to actually see in person. Many homes don't make the cut from the online glance to the actual showing.

You've worked hard to get to this point and your real estate agent should be getting your listing the right exposure. Once you have a qualified and interested buyer that wants to see your home, making access easy and accommodating showing requests will be the most important contribution a seller can make at this stage of the selling process.

Of course there are circumstances and exceptions to dropping everything and letting any and everyone into your home who wants to see your home. Agents that show buyers your home will typically not be wasting their own time without verifying the ability of said buyers to purchase your home, however there are the occasional tire kickers or "looky-loos" that are not serious about buying. Your agent should have steps in place to pre-screen showings to be sure that your showings are true buyers. At the end of the day, allowing as many qualified potential buyers see your home as possible will result in the most successful scenario for you as a seller.

One of the biggest mistake sellers make in the showing of their homes is actually being there. The seller should never be present during a showing. Neither the showing agent nor the buyer needs a guided tour of your home – even the most custom homes with unique features can be seen and sold without a helicoptering seller. While it may be hard to let go of this stage of the process, know that it is your best interest as a seller to not be present during showings and to allow the professional real estate agents show your home.

Three ways a seller "showing" the house can undermine a sale:

1. The buyer cannot openly express their desire to make the home their own such as changing paint colors,

repurposing a room, or redoing the kitchen thus not being able to see the potential.

2. The buyer feels like they are "intruding" and almost never stay as long as they would without the seller there.

3. The seller may offer information that may interfere with their agent's ability to negotiate later, should that buyer have interest in the home.

One of the many benefits of using a seasoned professional to represent you in the selling of your home is their negotiation skills and emotional detachment from the selling of your home. Your agent will be far better at fielding and answering questions from other real estate agents or potential buyers than you will be. Any questions a buyer has about your home after their showing can be addressed through the real estate agents.

Feedback, Secret Messages and Timing

Not every buyer will be a perfect match for your home. Getting feedback as to why your home was not right for a not interested buyer requires thick skin. If your home is not selling and the feedback is consistent and constructive, you and your agent should discuss making necessary changes based on that feedback, while at the same time reviewing overall marketing conditions since being on the market.

If there are showings, but no offers in a market where homes are selling within the same timeframe – or "Days on Market" – that your home is on the market, your agent should be able to get feedback from showings and from reviewing other market activity to help understand why your home stands out enough to be getting traffic, but not showing well enough to get an offer.

If you are not getting traffic in line with your market conditions, however, the issue is most likely price. Price is almost always the answer to a home not being shown. While location cannot be changed, price can be make the location more desirable. Lack of updates could be corrected (cost) or price adjusted to offset. Size cannot be easily changed, but price can be lowered to increase price-per-square foot.

Because the real estate market is impacted by so many outside factors, there are occasions where a seller will need to reposition their listing after being on the market. The key to continued success in these circumstances is knowing that time is of the essence and having a strategy to keep momentum.

The longer your home sits on the market, the less it will sell for. The current buyer pool will be exhausted having either seen your home online, in person or - if overpriced - not at all. These buyer that passed you by will have found another home and moved on. You are now a sitting duck waiting for new buyers to come on the market while competing with newer listings that have more appeal than one that gets the stigma of being passed over. Buyers ask three questions:

1. "How much is it?"
2. "How long on the market?"
3. "Why hasn't it sold?"

Because timing is important, be sure that you and your agent are cognizant of the timeline in your current market and are proactive in making any market adjustments so that you stay ahead of the market and not chasing it.

Where Buyers Come From

I cannot emphasize enough how each market is unique and when it comes to attracting buyers, each home is also a one-of-a-kind scenario. Most ready and willing buyers are typically pre-approved for financing and working with a real estate agent to find and purchase a home. Thus, marketing to real estate agents via the MLS remains the best way to reach a large number of buyers. The major real estate websites are also important to consider as buyers do start their searches online and most buyers are plugged into some type of automated search criteria feed. Since most of these sites pull their information from the local MLS data, your agent will be sure to be reaching those buyers as well. Everything else your agent does to market your home will work in concert to increase exposure to potential buyers and catch the attention of buyers on the fringe of your price point or location. Open houses are an example of an additional tool some real estate agents use that may or may not work in your market. While they are certainly an opportunity to get traffic through your home, they are not necessarily the magic pill that will sell your home quickly. Keep in mind that many attendees simply followed signs and balloons and don't even know your price point, whereas others are just starting their search and simply gathering research data to see how much house they can get for their money for a later purchase. There is also the security concern of having people through your home that may have ulterior motives. Most ready and able buyers prefer to see a home with their own agent rather than during crowded open houses, however open houses do allow buyers to come back for a second visit on their own. Your real estate agent can discuss the pros and cons of doing open houses and the success rate for your type of home and specific market.

Security Concerns

For the most part, people entering your home are doing so under good intentions. Criminals, however, will always take advantage of opportunity. The use of real estate agent-only lockboxes that provide more securely control access is extremely important and your real estate agent will provide this service for you. The technology surrounding these lockboxes let your real estate agent know who entered your property, when they were there and can identify who was the last person in your home. Most of the current lockboxes can also be set restrict access during specific times or days.

Keep in mind, most professional real estate agents value their time as well and will have done their due diligence in requiring potential buyers to be pre-approved for financing before showing them properties. This benefits you as a seller from the perspective of not having people through your home that are not qualified and that the extra step insures that they are legitimate buyers and not using the opportunity to be inside your home for nefarious reasons.

I always recommend taking additional necessary precautions with valuables and personal information to not provide any temptation. Here are a few general suggestions to consider while your home is on the market:

- Remove, lock up or store jewelry
- Put smaller electronics out of sight
- Make sure bills and statements are not left on in plain sight
- Remove extra house and car keys from wall hooks or obvious locations
- Remove or lock up any weapons
- Remove or lock up any prescription medications
- Remove décor with children's names and put away anything with school info
- Put away family calendars that show schedules and events when you will be gone

When you are on the market, the only thing you can expect it the unexpected. Your real estate professional has likely encountered numerous situations and is prepared for the unknown circumstances. You are dealing with the public in an open market, be prepared and trust the advice of your real estate agent.

Chapter Seven

Make Me an Offer I Can Refuse!

"During a negotiation, it would be wise not to take anything personally. If you leave personalities out of it, you will be able to see opportunities more objectively."

- Brian Koslow

Once on the market, sellers are typically anxious and eager to see an offer come in on their home. Too soon and the common reaction is that they priced their home too low. If they find themselves waiting for an offer, however, many sellers start to get insecure and panicked. The truth is that your current market environment should indicate the "Days on Market" or DOM for your home's location, price point and general features.

At the end of the day, you can only sell to one buyer. Sometimes they come right away, sometimes there is a little more time needed to make a match. The conditions of your local real estate market and how your home competes within that market determines the timeline and outcome.

As discussed, pricing should be in line with market value and preparation should be on point for maximum success in attracting buyers to your home. If this has been done properly and market conditions are favorable for selling, an offer should come in within the typical DOM for your home.

There are three important truisms to know and understand about offers:

1. Sellers control the marketing and pricing of the home, but buyers control market value.
2. The first offer is usually the best offer.
3. An offer is a sign of interest and willingness to buy.

Buyers Control Market Value

Your home is only worth what a buyer is willing to pay. Buyers will compare your home to what else is available in the market at that time and what they can get for the same amount of money. If a new construction home costs more money, but the buyer doesn't have to update or replace items, then the higher price home may be a better value. However, if your home has features or improvements that are appealing and is priced in line with similar sized homes in the same location, your home is the better value and will appeal to more buyers.

Because buyers will only be willing to pay for what they deem your home is worth to them, the amount a seller paid for the home or needs to net has no bearing on their perception of market value.

The First Offer is Usually the Best Offer

While there are exceptions of course, this is generally true for one key reason: the longer your home sits on the market, the less your home will sell for.

As buyers see and pass on your home – whether for reasons such as price, location, lack of features, etc. – those buyers will select other homes, leaving your home on the market with a higher DOM. As new buyers enter the market, they will likely look at the newer listed home first and then possibly see your home languishing on the market. Buyers will question why your home hasn't sold, wonder why other buyers passed it by and in some cases not even see your home as it falls further from the top of the stack. A "stale" listing then has to wait for new buyers to enter the market.

When you are a new listing, you will benefit by having the maximum amount of traffic both online and through your property. This is when you will attract the most amount of potential buyers and have your best chance at getting your best offer. Because of this, your first offer is typically your best offer. This is also when you will have a stronger opportunity to negotiate your highest price if the offer itself is not ideal.

An offer is a sign of interest

This is truly the most difficult moment in the transaction for many sellers. Negotiating, haggling and low-balling have negative connotations for most people - especially when it involves something this personal. The best advice I can give a seller is to NOT take it personal and trust the real estate professional they have hired to guide them through this process.

From a buyer's perspective, the purchase of your home is likely their biggest investment and they want to make sure they are not overpaying or leaving money on the table. Additionally, many buyers want to negotiate to ensure they are getting the best deal. The wild card is that you don't know your buyer, their negotiating style or where they are in the process of buying – starting low may be their strategy with the intention of paying full price or something close.

When an offer comes in lower than expected, the seller needs to focus on two things:

1. The purchaser has indicated they are interested in purchasing your home.
2. You don't know their bottom line based on their initial offer.

It is unlikely that a buyer took the time to schedule a showing, tour your listing, discuss the merits of your home, review comparable property data, discuss financing with a lender, consult with their real estate agent and then prepare, review and sign an offer if they were not interested in purchasing your home. While it varies from market-to-market, the process for a buyer to get to this point shows a sizable good faith commitment and interest in your home.

A buyer's offer is the first step in a mutual goal to a meeting of the minds, where the seller and a buyer agree to price and terms. Up to that point, a seller should expect an exchange back and forth as part of the negotiating process. In my experience, I have seen everything from parties starting so far apart that it appears unlikely they will be able to come together yet they do to the other extreme of buyers and sellers splitting hairs over a nominal amount, yet not being able to agree.

Both buyers and sellers often get emotional and attached to a specific number. It is here during the crucial negotiation stage that an experienced real estate professional on your side will be key to your success.

Tips for home sale negotiations:

1. Don't be offended by an offer – it is a starting point and is almost always higher than $0, as that is where you are starting from without an offer.
2. Don't get hung up on a number – whether it is what you want to get or what your neighbor got – market factors are simply sometimes out of your control.
3. Trust the real estate professional that you hired and listen to their guidance.
4. Look at the market factors as they pertain to your home.
5. Stay focused on the goal of selling your home.
6. Don't get emotional or make it personal – step back and let your real estate agent guide you.

Multiple Offers and Bidding Wars

Having multiple offers and a bidding war on your home is the Hollywood fantasy of every seller. While you can only sell to one buyer, the idea of attracting more than one is certainly appealing.

Let's look at some scenarios that could lead to possible multiple buyers interested in your property:

- **Inventory.**
  Supply and demand fluctuate – sometimes seasonal or other times related to different market factors. A shift in supply or lower inventory of homes can create a "seller's market". When there are more buyers than available homes, buyers become competitive in their offers and can be willing to do what it takes to make their offer more attractive.

- **Price.**
  As noted, over pricing your home will reduce the buyer pool due significantly. Buyers will either not even know your home is on the market when it doesn't show up in their search for similar properties or they will dismiss it as being priced high for the value. Pricing it at market value, however will attract prospective buyers looking for your type, size and price range of a home. If your home were to be priced below market – or market conditions were such that demand was higher than anticipated for your home – you would likely attract an even larger buyer pool. More exposure means more traffic which then leads to more interest and possibly additional offers.

- **Uniqueness.**
  An exceptional home that is also priced correctly – meaning in line with values rather than inflated to reflect what may be over-improvements – will attract more potential buyers due to the uniqueness. An example of this would be a home with custom features, additional structures, special location or upgrades that exceed what is typical in that market.

More buyers may mean more problems

While multiple offers often lead to a higher net to the seller and the ability to select better terms, there are some caution flags to consider when dealing with a bidding war. If you are experiencing market conditions that warrant multiple offers, it should be assumed that some of the buyers bidding on your property have experienced similar situations with other properties. With repeated losses in a competitive environment, some buyers may result to tricks to get their offer accepted. Your real estate professional will be key to navigating through the offers to determine which offer is truly the best offer. After all, if it doesn't make it to the closing or settlement table the price doesn't really matter. Some things to watch out for include buyers escalating their price beyond what a home would reasonable appraise for, leaving the seller ultimately selling for less or changing terms that are not in line with what their lender will allow or can accommodate.

Accepting an offer

Once you have reached a meeting of the minds, please be certain than you understand all of the terms and timelines you are agreeing to. In the speed to lock in the buyer or the price, don't be negligent in reading and understanding the contract prior to signing. While this seems obvious, the process of preparing a home for market, the vulnerability of being on the market and then the anxiety of the negotiation process leave many sellers just ready to be done.

Your real estate agent knows the contract you are signing and will guide you to how the contract protects the buyer and the seller in your market. Be certain you know what is expected of you, what conveys, what does not convey and the timelines you must adhere to. If there is language you do not understand or are not clear about the terms, consequences of not adhering to them or any other information, work with your real estate agent to source the answers to your questions and get the proper advice as it pertains to your situation.

Chapter Eight

The Road to the Finish Line

"It always seems impossible until it's done"

- Nelson Mandela

Congratulations - your home is under contract! While this is an exciting milestone in a seller's life, there is not time for the end zone celebration just yet. There are a series of major hurdles to pass in a short order. The period of time between accepting and offer and handing over the keys to the new owners will be a fast paced roller coaster ride.

As a reminder, every market is different in how each phase of a real estate transaction is handled - to the point of some calling this period "escrow" and others referring to it as being "under contract". The goal here is to help you have a general understanding of what a seller should expect during this important part of your transaction. The professional real estate agent you hired to get your home sold will be crucial in navigating the steps, avoiding the possible land mines and managing the rapid-fire details to get you to the finish line. This is where a good real estate agent will earn their keep and why you will be grateful you hired a professional.

While the actual settlement date would likely be negotiated and agreed upon in your sales contract, typically you can expect this to be a 30-45 day window. During this time period, there is a lot that has to happen to complete your sale. Among the many activities happening behind the scenes, this is when all of the various inspections and appraisals are conducted at your property. There will be numerous instances where other parties will need to have scheduled access to your home to keep the ball moving forward. Your cooperation with this is key to not hold up the process of the loan or miss important deadlines for removing buyer contingencies. A title search, land survey and obtaining your loan or other lien payoffs will also be taking place on your behalf. It is possibly that your involvement may be needed should a question or outstanding issue arise pertaining to these items. For the most part, however, your real estate agent and the appropriate third parties will be organizing and overseeing.

As the seller, you should be focused on these areas:

- Completing any agreed upon repairs and providing documentation as required.
- Maintaining your home so that it is delivered in same condition per your contract terms.
- Packing up your entire home so that you can be completely out on the date agreed upon.
- Adhering to timelines and deadlines agreed to in your contract.

Home Inspection

The home inspection stage of the transaction is often a nail biter for most sellers, most likely due to feeling vulnerable and the fear of the unknown. When put under the scrutiny of an inspector's magnifying glass, even the most well-maintained home will likely have issues discovered that the sellers would not have been aware of.

The purpose of the home inspection is three-fold:

1. To educate the buyer on the workings, maintenance and future concerns of the home.
2. To determine if there are any major issues that would preclude the buyer from moving forward with the purchase.
3. To identify defects that the buyer would like to negotiate with the seller to correct as part of the agreement, possibly voiding the contract if not agreed upon.

While each buyer is unique in their expectations, your real estate agent will be key in guiding you through the process of negotiating the terms of your home inspection agreement to include what is typical and reasonable in your market for a seller to address.

Other inspections vary by market, but you may also have inspections for radon, lead paint, wood destroying insects or other environmental issues.

Be certain that you are clear as to what the buyer's expectation is for any repairs you are agreeing to make so that you are meeting your contractual obligations and there are no last minute surprises later.

Appraisal

While sellers fret over the home inspection, most agents know that the appraisal is the steepest hurdle. It is often said that a real estate agent must sell a home twice: first to a buyer and second to an appraiser. The appraiser is hired by the buyer's lender to provide an unbiased, third party professional opinion as to whether the home's value is at or above the contract sales price. That's right – the appraiser typically has a copy of the contract between you and the buyer in hand and knows what the contract price is, type of financing and any concessions or credits given back to the buyer. The appraiser is not looking to assign a value to your home, but simply making sure the collateral (your home) is equal or greater in value to sales price (not loan amount) used to calculate the loan to value of the buyer's mortgage amount. In other words, is the house worth the price the buyer is paying?

Appraisers will visit the home, measure square footage, take pictures, verify improvements and overall condition, and determine the value based on features of your home compared to recently sold similar homes. The process involves a visit to the property, research and a report that is sent to the lender directly. Sellers rarely see the appraisal or know the actual value unless the value comes in under the contract price. In this case, if the sale is subject to a satisfactory appraisal, one of these courses of action usually take place:

- Parties agree to move forward with the sales price being the appraised value.
- Parties negotiate the buyer paying part or all of the difference between the contract price and the appraised price in cash.
- The contract is mutually voided by both parties.

The best way to avoid having an issue with a low appraisal is to properly price the home from the start and be realistic in expectations on sales price.

Final Walkthrough

Prior to the final settlement or closing, the buyers along with their agent will want to visit the property to conduct a final walkthrough. This should be scheduled near the date of your closing, but not necessarily the same day in case there are any issues that arise.

The purpose of the buyer's final walkthrough is:

- To verify the home inspection repair items have been completed.
- The home is in the agreed upon condition.
- There has not been a material change to the home.
- All agreed upon items of conveyance are still present.

The seller's obligation is to deliver the home to the buyer as agreed. The expectation is that the home would be in that condition at the time of the final walkthrough. Your real estate agent would work with the buyer's real estate agent to quickly resolve any discrepancies as to not delay settlement.

Settlement or Closing

The final act in your transaction is the closing of the sale. The expectation should be that this is an uneventful moment in the transaction. All negotiations and discrepancies should be well resolved prior to this day.

Getting you and the entire transaction to this point is the most important role of your real estate agent. At this point, all contingencies should be removed and the buyer's loan should be cleared to close. Your real estate agent will have worked with you to manage checking off all of the boxes to be sure every required task has been completed to get to this point. All that is left is to sign the deed and other required documents transferring ownership, as well as closing out and paying off your liens. Because each market is different, I won't go into the specifics of the actual settlement or closing. Your real estate agent will guide you up to this point and then is typically present during settlement to assist in going over the documents with you and that they represent the terms of the contract.

Loose Ends

Over the course of the weeks leading up to the closing or settlement, most sellers are preoccupied with packing and moving logistics. In addition, sellers and their real estate agents are also typically focused on wrapping up and documenting home inspection repairs to meet the requirements of the contract. With all of the distractions, it is easy to overlook some important details.

Here are a few reminders:

- Be sure to notify to post office and any automatic deliveries of your change of address well in advance of your move to allow time for mail and packages enroute to be properly forwarded.
- Stop all automatic payments such as mortgage or home owner association dues prior to settlement.
- Collect all keys from baby sitters, dog walkers, etc.
- Cancel or transfer all maintenance contracts that are not part of the sale.
- Do keep all insurance in place until after settlement.

So Many Moving Parts

There is rarely anything simple about selling a home and the path from start to finish is often a bumpy one. Knowledge and experience are the two key skills your real estate agent brings to the table. With this likely being one of the largest transactions you'll ever experience, having a steep learning curve while you work through trial and error on your own may cost you money, time or both. Trust in a professional that knows how to guide you through decisions and manage the numerous facets of your transaction.

Chapter Nine

The Upside Down Turnaround

"A bank is a place that will lend you money if you can prove that you don't need it"

\- Bob Hope

Unfortunately, there are rare situations where sellers are what we call "upside down" in their mortgage. This occurs when they owe more on their mortgage(s) than the amount they can sell their home. Because the real estate value fluctuates similar to the stock market, home values are always changing. When a seller needs to sell their home when they have not been in their home long enough to build equity or the values are lower than at the time the purchased, distress selling is something that is considered.

Since a home is a tremendous long-term investment, the first consideration should be given to keeping any capital and equity intact. Do you absolutely "have" to move or is this a "want"? If not paramount, then staying in the home to build more equity and allow market conditions to improve would be ideal.

If moving is unavoidable, then looking at renting out your property should be heavily considered as your first option. Owning investment property may not have been your initial goal, but the long term benefits of building equity, creating a nest-egg and essentially letting someone else pay down your mortgage each month while you keep they investment is an excellent way to build long-term wealth. An experienced real estate agent can guide you with information and likely find you a suitable tenant.

Short Sales and Foreclosures

Should your extreme circumstances not benefit from either of the above solutions, then a distress sale may be the best solution for you. The information provided here is simply an overview of these particular options. You should consult an experienced real estate agent in your market, an attorney, your bank or lending institution and a tax advisor to fully understand the financial, legal and tax consequences surrounding a distress sale.

A "Short Sale" is the lessor of the two evils. This process is initiated by the homeowner in an effort to avoid foreclosing on their home. The homeowner remains in the property and sells the home using the services of a real estate agent in generally the same manner as if they were selling traditionally. The home is advertised as a potential short sale and that the sale would be subject to the approval of a third party – which would be the lien holder or lender. This requires the seller to heavily document to their lender their unavoidable reasons for needing to short sale, which would typically involve work, health, and/or financial dire straits. There is usually nothing "short" about a short sale as it generally takes a longer timeframe and the sale can sometimes in the end not even be approved by the lender. All of this uncertainty is unappealing to most ready and willing buyers. As a result, the home is typically sold for less than market value as an enticement to buyers willing to be flexible and wait for the lender's decision.

A "foreclosure" is a legal process where the lender or bank takes possession of the property after the homeowner defaults on their loan repayment obligations. The bank forces the sale of the asset (the property) to recover the balance owed to them.

Choosing to either short sale or foreclose on your home has both short and long term consequences to your personal credit and may have additional tax consequences. It is important that you know what the penalties are beforehand from a trusted professional who is an expert in this area.

Early Intervention

Life throws the occasional curve ball causing financial and personal situations to change from that joyous day when you first purchased your home. Know that there are numerous resources available to assist homeowners find appropriate solutions to keep their home, credit and financial security intact.

First and foremost, communicate with your lender and be proactive in finding a solution early. There are legitimate programs available to assist most home owners, however don't sign anything or enter into any agreement without the assistance of a trusted advisor to be certain it is the right solution for you. After all, if you cannot pay your current mortgage, adding a second loan will not be any easier.

Here is a list of resources should you need advice or assistance:

> Most homeowners can contact the US Department of Housing and Urban Development (HUD)800-569-4287 to find a HUD Mortgage Counselor in your area

> Homeowners with an FHA-insured loan should contact The US Department of Housing and Urban Development (HUD) National Servicing Center at 1-877-622-8525

Appendix I

This flow chart shows a very generalized timeline of what to expect while in selling your home. A lot has to happen both in front of you and behind the scenes for a successful sale. Some stages the seller has control and at other times it is the buyer or the market in general at the helm.

While your real estate agent will outline the more specific tasks and expectations at each juncture, this chart gives you an idea of the importance of planning and being prepared for a fast paced journey to the finish line.

Seller Timeline

- Interview & Select Real Estate Agent
- Determine if costs to sell allow you to proceed
- Know where you will be moving and/or alternate plans
- Make repairs/improvements to home
- Declutter/stage home
- Determine listing price based on market data
- Home is listed for sale
- Make home available to be shown
- Review offers with real estate agent and negotiate
- Read and understand all terms of an offer before accepting
- Once under contract, make home available for various inspections
- Complete any required repairs and document
- Pack and arrange for movers

Appendix II

Costs of Selling Worksheet

PREPARATION STAGE:		
	Repair Cost Estimates (plumbing, electrical, exterior trim, etc.)	$
	Replacement Cost Estimates (worn carpet, broken appliances, etc.)	$
	Home Prep (mulch, paint, etc.)	$
	Decluttering (boxes, storage unit, etc.)	$
INSPECTION STAGE:		
	Required Seller-Paid Inspections*	$
	Required Repair Budget	$
	Negotiated Repair Budget	
SALE STAGE:		
	Payoff of ALL Existing Liens	
	Real Estate Commissions*	$
	Taxes Paid As Part of Sale*	$
	Recording/Government Fees*	$
	Attorney or Settlement Fees*	$
	Pro-Rated Real Estate Taxes	
	Other*	$
TOTAL ESTIMATE COST OF SELLING*		**$**

*Your local Real Estate agent will be able to provide more specific information for your market. This is intended to provide a very generalized idea of the additional costs of selling a home and is for informational purposes only. Please consult an expert in your area for actual costs.

About The Author

Traci Oliver is highly regarded real estate professional, licensed to practice in The Commonwealth of Virginia. She is a Realtor-member of The National Association of Realtors, Northern Virginia Association of Realtors and is currently affiliated with TTR Sotheby's International Realty. Traci is a consistent top producing, high-volume real  estate agent who has received numerous industry awards recognizing her successes. She is highly ranked and reviewed on nearly all online real estate websites, as well as by notable regional and national publications, earning the highest recognition for her esteemed accomplishments in the real estate field.

Licensed in 2001, Ms. Oliver has experienced all types of real estate markets, yet her real estate business has remained strong throughout her career due to her professional approach, consistent work ethic and tried-and-true methods.

In addition to her successful real estate practice, Ms. Oliver has conducted numerous first-time buyer seminars to educate potential buyers about the market and the home buying process. She is also a frequent presenter, training other real estate agents and groups on the subjects of marketing, networking, real estate business generation, communicating to sellers and the art of working with buyers and sellers.

Traci is a native to the Washington DC suburbs and currently resides in Northern Virginia with her husband, daughter and rescue dog.